Westward in a Trunk

By Michala Miller

Western Reflections Publishing Company®

Lake City, Colorado

ISBN 978-1-937851-15-6

Cover photo by Pat and Mary Haverfeld
All other photos are property of the author and her family.
Cover and book design: Laurie Goralka Design

First Edition
Printed in the United States of America

Western Reflections Publishing Company®
P.O. Box 1149, 951 N. Highway 149
Lake City, CO 81235
(970) 944-0110
publisher@westernreflectionspublishing.com
www.westernreflectionspublishing.com

Dedicated to all of Michala's numerous friends.

Without the efforts of Harriet, Chet & Carole, Cousin Nancy, and the Steamboat Writer's Group along with the encouragement and enthusiasm of countless others, you would not be holding this book!

Many thanks to Pat & Mary Haverfield for the professional photographs of Harmettio.

FOREWARD

Michala Miller, our mother, completed this, her second book, shortly after requiring ongoing round-the-clock care for a progressive but never diagnosed disease. During the difficult eight months that followed, Mom never lost hope, right up to her last breath. She hoped that she would get well and she hoped that this book would be published. Typical, though, of her and our father, she had a back-up plan. If no publisher was interested in the manuscript, she herself would print enough copies for everyone in the family!

a dozen boxes, she found the china-headed dolls, tucked side by side, layer after layer. Not just any doll would do. She searched for that certain one. She was almost to the bottom of the box when Lula found what she'd come for. She held the small doll up in the dim light to examine it. Yes, this was the one. The light colored hair, the blue eyes, and the rosy cheeks were just as she had remembered. "You are a pretty lady. I'm so glad no one bought you last Christmas." She put all the black-haired dolls back, placed the cover on the box and closed the door. When she got to the front of the store she laid the doll on the counter. Lula's father tore a piece of paper from the big, brown roll. "I see that you picked the one with the yellow hair for your daughter." His eyes twinkled, his smile broad, and he couldn't help but chuckle.

"Yes," she replied, "It will match Ethel's hair."

Her father laughed loudly. "What hair? All she has is a little white fuzz."

"By the time she's six months old she'll have blond curls," promised Lula.

"Does the baby get it now?" Her father asked, "She's too young to play with a doll and it's a long time until December."

Lula said, "I don't want to wait until Christmas. I want Ethel to have this one today.

It is two dollars, isn't it?"

He nodded as he wrapped the paper loosely around the little doll, and tied the package with a string.

Lula left the store and walked to the comer. She stepped down from the wooden sidewalk and turned onto the street that went towards the river. Almost running, she finally paused to catch her breath and look at the big river that flowed before her.

The Ohio River had come nearly nine hundred miles from its beginning in Pennsylvania. It was now wide and deep as it flowed past Elizabethtown, Illinois. Across the river was the state of Kentucky and within less than a hundred miles the Ohio's journey would end when the mighty Ohio joined the mightier Mississippi River.

William and Hirametta Birch, Ethel's grandparents, in front of Ethel's parent's home–originally a boarding house.

But this day Lula didn't linger to admire the river or watch the barges as they floated by. Her thoughts rested on the gift tucked under her arm. The gate banged behind her as she hurried up the walk and into the large, red-brick house. "Alice, Alice," she called, "Come see what I have!" She ripped away the paper.

Alice and her little boy had come to do the laundry and watch Ethel while Lula ran errands. Alice put the iron back on the stove to stay hot and turned to look at the doll. "My, oh my, would you look at this?" She reached out to hold the doll and cradle it in her strong arms. "Get off those stairs, Henry, and come see." Five-year old Henry grabbed the banister knob and swung out over the bottom three steps.

"Isn't she beautiful? You may touch her, but gently."

Henry touched the doll's head. He was more interested, however, in a glass foot that hung down below the ice blue dress. He inspected the brown, painted-on shoe that was no bigger than a dime and the white hose above it. But most of all he stared at the painted blue garter that was tied with a painted bow and peeked out just below the pantaloon. Henry lifted the dress to see if there were two feet and fingered both of them. What funny looking shoes and stockings!

"Miss Lula, she is the prettiest doll," said Alice.

"I call her Pretty Lady," said Lula, "Let's go give the doll to Ethel right now. We won't wake her."

The three tiptoed to the bedside and Lula propped the doll up with a pillow. Henry stared down at the baby with white fuzz for hair. "She's too little to play with a doll. She can't even roll over."

Alice said, "This doll isn't just for now, Henry. This is Ethel's doll forever."

For months, Pretty Lady sat either in a corner of the crib or on top of the tall dresser. Every week Alice dusted her china head, held her in her arms and spread out her gathered skirt. A few times Henry admired the doll, but it wasn't long before he started school and forgot all about the painted-on shoes.

Ethel grew, learned to walk and talk, and to say, "My doll." The days, months, and years came and went. One warm fall day, when Ethel was six years old and big oak leaves fell to the ground, she sat on the porch swing with her friend Daisy. They rocked their dolls back and forth.

"Why do you call her Pretty Lady?'

"My mother named her," said Ethel.

Daisy said, "She needs a real name, like Pearl. My favorite aunt is called Pearl."

"My grandma's name is Hiramette. I love my grandmother." Ethel thought and thought. "My doll is going to have a name that's different from any doll's name in the whole world." She thought some more. Suddenly she hugged her doll. "Her name is Harmettio."

"What a funny name!" Daisy giggled, "No one has that name."

"My doll does."

An early childhood portrait of Ethel, Harmettio's first owner.

2

Fireflies
1907

Ethel let the screen door bang on purpose. She was glad this day was over. It was her grandmother's birthday and they had spent the entire day out at her grandparents' farm. Usually a trip to the farm meant playing with cousins, climbing trees, and straddling the big, gray workhorse. But for Grandmother Birch's birthday, her seven children were assembled with all their young ones, and a real photographer had come from town to take everyone's picture. To Ethel, the family picture meant wearing her "go to church" dress, having her hair curled on rags the night before, then combed back and tied with a velvet ribbon. If all that wasn't bad enough, she had to wear shoes. Why should she wear shoes? No one could see her feet when they were all lined up for the camera.

For some photographs she sat on the grass with all the cousins and smiled for the camera. Sometimes she stood in front of her mother and smiled, and once she was in the second row for a picture of Grandmother and all the grandchildren. Ethel was sure her shoes never showed. To show her disapproval, she shuffled her feet back and forth all day. Ethel hated shoes.

At dinner her mother had whispered, "Sit proper and keep your feet still." Now that they were home she wanted to take her shoes off but her mother warned her, "Leave them on so your feet are clean when you crawl into bed."

Ethel stomped across the porch to the steps where she sat down with Harmettio. She smoothed her skirt so that the doll lay across her lap as if she were in a hammock.

From the falling dusk and just up the street, she heard her friend, Daisy, call, "Get a jar, Ethel, and come catch fireflies." Daisy's sister, Olive, chimed in, "They're out good tonight. Hurry! We have to go in soon."

A family portrait of Ethel with her parents, Lula and Oscar Bruce, taken about 1906.

Ethel hadn't been paying attention to the tiny flickering lights. She had been thinking about a whole day of wearing shoes when it wasn't even school time. Now she noticed the fireflies darting around the honeysuckle bushes, their lamps flashing like lighthouses warning any approaching ship of a dangerous, rocky point.

"Come inside my gate," Ethel yelled, as she jumped up to join in the fun. "There's a peck of them sparking around the bushes." She called through the open door, "Ma, hey Ma! I need a jar. I'm going to catch fireflies!"

Harmettio lay forgotten on the second step where she'd fallen from Ethel's lap.

The Kersey sisters came up the walk. "Look at our jars." Sure enough, lights flickered on and off, almost like a lantern.

"I have more than you," said Daisy, as she held her jar up for inspection.

Olive disagreed, "No you don't. Look at all of mine light up."

There might have been more arguing, but Mother Lula stepped out onto the porch carrying a Mason jar. She leaned forward to peer at the owners of the blinking lights. "Hello girls."

Together the girls said, "Evening, Ma'am." The Kersey sisters frequently spoke in unison. Maybe it was because their mother dressed them alike. Both had pigtails, and they went everywhere together. Olive was a year older but no taller than her sister. "We're not twins," she told everyone, "I'm much older."

And Daisy always added, "By just ONE year."

Ethel jumped off the porch, knelt on the grass and opened her jar. Many fireflies hovered close to the ground, blinking off and on. She knew the secret to catching them. First she spotted one while the light was on, then quickly trapped it in her cupped hands before the bug's taillight switched off, and it disappeared into the dark.

"Here's one." Ethel popped her hands together over the unsuspecting firefly. She lifted one finger and peeked inside. "Missed!" She tried again, and before long her jar was twinkling as brightly as her friends'.

The night was filled with tiny lights, the sweet smell of the honeysuckles and the sound of jar lids being screwed off and on. A voice from the dark called, "Kersey girls, come home!"

"Coming Ma'am," two voices replied. Olive and Daisy were known all over Elizabethtown for their politeness. "We have to go."

"I know," said Ethel, "Are you going to turn them loose?"

"Yes," said Daisy, "Mother doesn't like fireflies in the house."

"And they just die if you leave them in the jar," added Olive.

"Let's wait until we get home." Daisy giggled, "They'll light our way." They lived just four houses down on the other side of the street. The gate squeaked behind the sisters as they called their goodbyes. Holding their jar high, they disappeared.

Ethel climbed the porch steps to show her mother her firefly collection. Suddenly there was a crunching sound! It came from beneath her shoe. "Oh, no!" she cried as she dropped the jar to feel over and around the step. Her throat hurt. "Oh no! Mother!" She pulled her doll up by her skirt and raced inside. In the light she examined Harmettio. Where there used to be a tiny glass hand, a stump of stuffed material hung down. Sawdust dribbled out. Tears spilled over Ethel's cheeks and splashed down onto the doll's blue dress. "Look Mother, come see what I've done."

After seeing Harmettio, Lula tried to console her daughter, but a heartbroken Ethel stumbled off to bed where she cried herself to sleep.

The next morning they found pieces of the crushed hand. They were too small to glue together. Mother sewed the dangling wrist shut to keep the sawdust from leaking out. Then she placed the doll on top of the dresser drawers and fluffed out Harmettio's skirt to hide the place where a hand used to be.

Ethel's eyes were red and swollen from crying. Putting a wet rag over her eyes, she stayed inside so no one would see her. She soon grew tired of holding the cloth before her face and tossed it beside the wash basin. Ethel wandered outside to help shell peas. As she pried the pods apart, she asked herself, "How could I hurt my doll, how could I?" When she had finished shelling, she placed the dish alongside the water pump and went to her room where she cradled Harmettio in her arms. She tucked the handless arm in the folds of her shirt, cupped her hand around the glass head and rocked back and forth on the bed.

When Alice came to clean she looked sadly at Harmettio, but tried to sound cheerful.

"Those things happen. They just happen."

But Ethel knew better, her Pretty Lady wasn't as pretty anymore.

3

The Flood Comes

"Rain, Rain! Rain," Ethel muttered, "Nothing but rain: I hate rain." She stood looking out of the tall, narrow parlor window. She didn't notice the muddy street filled with puddles and the streams of water trickling toward the river. Ethel did notice the Ohio River that was rising to meet them, pressing against its banks, persistent and angry. It always rained in the spring and the river always grew in size; but as she stared at all the water she thought, this time it's different.

Just three days before, Ethel and her mother had huddled under the black, silk umbrella and sloshed to the General Store. They had stood among the farmers and town folk and listened to the talk—talk of flooding. "The river is up seven feet," said the blacksmith.

Grandfather from his usual place behind the counter added, "They're sand bagging day and night, all along the river."

"We need to do more," said the constable. "This could be a bad one."

Several echoed, "Very bad."

Ethel had never seen a flood but she'd heard about them. Elizabethtown had flooded in the past, before she was born. The town sat on a bluff overlooking the river. The houses always seemed high above the water. Now the dark, churning river lapped closer and closer to the brink of the hill. On the way home from the store, Ethel had asked her mother, "Do you ever remember the river flooding?"

"Do I! Once when I was about your age the river rose, and spread out over the land. Friends and relatives that lived in the town came to stay with us at the farm. I thought it was like a party to have children to play with, but it was a sad time. Some people lost everything they owned."

Ethel turned away and hurried to her room. She didn't want to think about floods.

The river was unfriendly, scary. She lifted Harmettio down from her place on the dresser and climbed up on her bed. The thick feather mattress settled around them like a safe cocoon. Whenever Ethel felt sad or a little frightened, she liked to burrow down in her soft bed and hide from the world. This was such a day. She had just settled in when there was a banging on their front door and voices shouting from the street.

"River's rising! River's rising!"

The Baptist Church at Elizabethtown during a flood in the 1910s.

Mother answered the door and talked briefly to whoever stood on the other side.

When the door shut she called out, "Ethel, come quickly!"

Ethel was already struggling to her feet. She didn't even take time to put her doll up or smooth the deep dent they'd made in the bed.

"We must move whatever we can upstairs. Take your shoes, books, everything on the floor in your room. Everything the water can hurt, and, here, take these pillows!" Mother was talking fast and moving even faster around the room gathering an armload as she headed for the stairs.

"Is the river coming into our house?" asked Ethel. It was all so confusing. "Where's Father?" she howled.

Mother called back over her shoulder, "Don't be dilatory, Ethel, your father is stacking sandbags. Now hurry!"

Ethel choked back fears and tears as she picked up her shoes, a stack of books from the corner, and her china tea set. It took three trips just to get all of the books to safety. She put her things in an empty room at the end of the upstairs hall. It had the musty smell of a place seldom used. As soon as she got back downstairs her mother had another load for her. Four trips, five, and then six, up and down she trudged until Ethel lost count. Her legs ached, her arms ached. She ached all over.

"Take these linens and the Bible and ... "

"Are we going to wash away?" she asked.

Mother put down her load and wrapped her arms around Ethel "Of course not, we're just going to live upstairs. We may not even get any water in our home."

Ethel looked out of the window for the first time in several hours. She saw that the end of the street had disappeared into the encroaching water, and water was washing over the sandbags. It was all happening so quickly.

As they were moving more things upstairs, Father came in and began pulling out dresser drawers. He hauled them to the second floor or stacked them on top of tables. His clothes were soaked, and his wet felt hat drooped down about his face. He didn't even take it off, and his boots spilled muddy puddles throughout the house and up the stairs. No one was expecting company or a clean floor at a time like this. The river was rising.

Before Father returned to the brow of the hill to stack more burlap bags, he folded the feather mattresses and lugged them upstairs. He laid Ethel's on the floor in the back room. They would all have dry beds.

Ethel put her pillow in place and covered her bed with a blanket. She was so tired she didn't wait for Mother to say, "Bedtime," or to even take off her clothes. She just sank onto the floor and crawled under her blanket. The rain drummed against the house. The entire world is wet, she thought.

When Ethel awoke she looked for her dresser and Harmettio but there was no dresser at the foot of her bed and no doll. "Harmettio, where's Harmettio?" Ethel bolted upright. She frantically felt around her mattress! She lifted her blanket and shook it. "Ma, I can't find Harmettio."

Ethel's grandfather on a ladder during the flood.

There was no answer. Then she remembered that she was upstairs. She rolled out onto her knees, stood up and padded down the long hall. Ethel was half way down the stairs when she saw the water. The floor was covered with water! "Mother," she cried, "Where are you?"

Lula came splashing in from the kitchen. She climbed up the few steps to Ethel, and hugged her.

"How deep is it?" Ethel's voice sounded weak and squeaky. It sounded like she might cry.

"It's only five or six inches," said Mother, "but it will get deeper. Nothing can hold back the river this time."

"Where's Father?" Ethel tried to gulp back the tears.

Mother squeezed her shoulder, "He's been out all night. They are moving the older people to higher ground."

"What about Grandfather and Grandmother?"

"Their farm is higher and, besides, Uncle Will is out there."

Ethel leaned against Lula. "I can't find Harmettio."

"She must be somewhere upstairs," said Mother and went to look. They searched among the piles of clothes, the stacks of dishes, the bags of flour, beans, rice, even the books, Mother's crocheting and her quilt pieces. They looked everywhere.

They went downstairs and began to search again. Ethel waded in the dirty water. She felt the wet floorboards beneath her feet as she went from room to room. Then she remembered she had left her doll on her bed. Ethel sloshed into her room and knelt alongside the bed frame. She ran

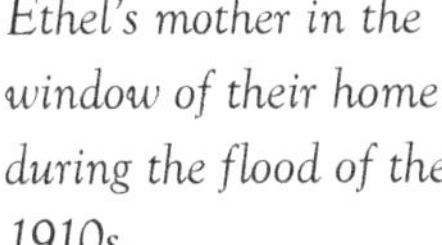

Ethel's mother in the window of their home during the flood of the 1910s.

her fingers through the water until they touched the floor beneath. Her hands swished back and forth until her fingers struck something round and slick. She lifted Harmettio out of the water by her head. The doll's clothes were a dirty, soggy mess. Her head was smudged with mud. The cloth body with the sawdust inside was wet and heavy. One of her tiny feet was missing. Gone! Maybe it was close by? Ethel groped around, and let the murky water fan through her fingers, but she felt nothing. The foot was gone. It must have washed somewhere in the house. When the flood's over, I'll find it. Ethel felt sure of that.

More rain came. Levees, weakened by the river's force, crumbled and slid into the rolling water. Trees, bobbing and turning, washed past. The river stretched everywhere.

Every so often, Ethel measured the water depth in the house with the handle of a broom. She leaned over the stair railing pushing the handle downward until it hit the floor below. Five inches, eight inches, a foot, two feet, soon the water came up to the broom's straw and Ethel quit measuring. Instead she spent hours reading and looking out of the windows.

On Sunday morning Ethel heard her grandfather's, "Hello! Anyone home?" She rushed to the front window anxious to see him. She was so glad to hear his voice.

Grandfather was below in a rowboat. A gray and dull sky lingered, but it wasn't raining. The little boat rocked and bumped against the house.

Lula leaned out of the window. "We're here," she laughed, "Where can we go?" She asked about family and friends.

"How about Daisy and Olive?" asked Ethel "Have you seen them?"

Grandfather hadn't heard about her friends but added, "Probably doing well. Most people in two story houses are fine."

"What about the store," asked Mother? The Birch General Store was on higher ground than their home and it sat on a tall, rock foundation.

"We have two feet or better inside, but we got the bolts of cloth, the flour sacks and sugar bins upstairs. We lost everything on the bottom shelves."

"Any news from upriver?" asked Mother.

"Word is the river's crested at Grayville. It will soon start dropping."

That was exciting news to Ethel. She felt like a prisoner, an upstairs prisoner.

Besides she was sure she'd find Harmettio's foot as soon as the river returned to its banks. Ethel did not know that when the river's rampage ended, it left behind destruction.

The river receded. It had been a long time since Ethel had seen the ground, the sidewalk, or the porch. Her room smelled of mud, rotting wood and garbage. Even with all the windows and doors open, the paint peeled, and the floor, covered with gooey mud, was soggy underfoot. Everyone along the river shoveled out the debris, scraped, washed, and painted. Their world slowly dried out.

Ethel hauled all her things downstairs to her room, put Harmettio back on the dresser, sat her tea set on the round table in the corner, and stacked her books everywhere. She was glad to hear the gate squeak and see the Kersey girls again. It was a happy time for everyone except Harmettio. Ethel never found the lost foot.

4

Lightning
1918

Ethel placed her doll beside her comb and brush. "Are you glad I'm home, Harmettio?" When she left for college she left her doll in her usual place on the dresser. Ethel rubbed her fingers lightly over the rosy-painted cheeks. Then she turned toward the bed where Daisy sat unpacking her friend's satchels.

"I don't understand why you went so far away to school. I missed you," said Daisy.

"I've only been gone nine months, and I came home for Christmas," said Ethel.

"Besides, I want to teach. I've wanted to be a teacher for as long as I can remember."

"You never even liked school," Daisy protested.

Ethel thought for a minute. "I didn't dislike school. I just got tired of sitting still."

Ethel had come home for the summer from college some eighty miles away. It was a school for those studying to be teachers. She liked the school's big, red, brick buildings laced with ivy, and the winding paths throughout the campus.

Ethel was nineteen-years old. Taller than most of the young ladies in her class, she had long, thick, auburn hair, and soft brown eyes. No one ever called her dainty or fragile, but she was pretty and quite headstrong. Quilting and knitting were not for Ethel. "Please Mother," she often said, "don't ever ask me to go to the sewing club." She much preferred to swim and fish, explore the caves along the river, and target shoot with her boy cousins.

Mother Lula had long ago given up on telling her to be proper.

During Ethel's college vacation she earned money for school by helping Grandfather Birch in the general store. "It's good to have you home," Grandfather had said. "I've had no one to tease."

Ethel stocked the shelves, the thread drawers, the shoe table, and even filled the pickle barrel. She swept the floors, feather dusted the canned goods, and when the store was busy, she helped wait on the customers. She loved measuring and cutting the grosgrain ribbon from their long rolls, but she hated to fill the brown paper bags with eggs. They cracked so easily.

"When you're here I have to order twice as many eggs from the farmers," said Grandfather.

"Not that many," said Ethel.

Grandfather laughed, "I'd break all the eggs just to have you home with me."

Ethel smiled and hugged the man with the twinkling eyes.

In the evenings Ethel and Daisy strolled down Walnut Street to see Daisy's sister, Olive, who was now married, and had a baby boy. She lived in a little house dwarfed by two tall trees. Olive planted a big garden and grew the finest tomatoes in all of Elizabethtown.

Daisy had a boyfriend that worked at the post office. "Sam's a hard worker and he likes all the Kersey family, especially Olive's baby," she said. Daisy loved being an aunt and insisted on holding baby William. "Isn't he just precious?" Ethel agreed although she wished she got a turn holding the baby.

"He's a beautiful baby," purred Daisy.

Ethel nodded in agreement.

Daisy announced, "When I get married I want a baby just like William."

By mid-summer Ethel grew tired of hearing about Olive's baby and Daisy's beau.

She wanted to talk about her classes, the books she'd read, and the friends she'd made at college. After work one evening Ethel strolled alone along the river. As she walked along its banks she gazed at the barges and boats that floated past. Sometimes she waved at the river pilots, and sometimes they waved back.

It's a hot, sticky summer, thought Ethel. She had seen the men mop their brows with large, square handkerchiefs, while the women waved straw fans before their faces. All everyone talked about was the weather. Isn't there anything else to discuss, she wondered?

Later, when Ethel got home, she threw her pillow down on the floor beside her bed. She often slept there where it was cooler than lying on her feather mattress.

A black, ugly storm covered the sky. The sound of thunder rolled in from the distance, growing louder as it approached. Soon a welcome breeze wafted in the window, and for the first time in many nights, Ethel climbed back into her bed. It felt so good to lie there. She quickly fell asleep.

The rumblings grew louder. A strong wind blew the curtains away from the open window. Flashes of light filled Ethel's room but she slept on until she heard a frightening, crackling sound. The house lurched! Ethel was thrown from her bed! She lit with a thud! Her dresser tumbled over and Harmettio crashed to the floor.

"What's happened?" Ethel yelled. She jumped up, rubbed her shoulder and sniffed the air. A strange burning smell filled the room.

Her father appeared in the doorway. In a flash of light she could see that he had pulled his pants on over his nightshirt. "You all right?" he asked her.

"Yes Pa, but what happened?"

Her father was already half way up the stairs and didn't answer. Ethel followed.

When she got to the second floor the hall was full of smoke. The house was on fire. Her legs trembled, her eyes burned, and she couldn't stop coughing.

Father pulled down the trap door to the attic. Water rushed into the hallway. He climbed the ladder and disappeared into the attic darkness. Ethel stared up. Just then there was another flash and she saw a big hole in the roof. Fire lashed upward to meet the rain and flames licked at the rafters. Lightning! Their house had been struck! Rain poured in through the gaping hole.

Ethel heard talking on the stairs and recognized the voices of Alice and Henry. "I knew someone had been hit," said Henry, "It had to be close."

They joined Ethel. Henry called up into the attic, "How can I help?"

"I need boards, nails and a hammer," answered Father, "and Ethel, get some buckets and more help."

He had hardly spoken when they heard the sound of other folks on the porch. Ethel flew down the steps to get buckets and open the door for Olive and Daisy's father and brothers.

They worked through the night. Henry climbed into the attic to help Father nail up the boards that the Kerseys handed up to them. The women dipped burlap bags into the water buckets. When wet they were handed to other waiting hands. A slapping sound came from above as the sacks smacked against the burning attic walls. The rain did its part by pelting the roof and drowning out the fire. All the while Ethel mopped up the stream of water that filled the hallway and threatened to cascade down the stairs.

At morning's first light the rain stopped, a makeshift roof was in place, and the flames extinguished. Ethel walked wearily to her room. All she wanted was to stretch out on her bed and sleep and sleep. She stopped short when she saw her dresser lying on its side. She grabbed the top and tugged. It was very heavy. She braced her shoulder against the drawers and heaved it upward into place. Alongside the dresser lay Harmettio. Ethel knew her doll was smashed. Gingerly she lifted her, turned her over and over checking for chips, cracks, holes or tears. The doll with one hand and one foot was just fine.

"You are a Lucky Lady," said Ethel as she placed Harmettio back on the dresser, and crawled into bed. Far away, lightening still flashed, and thunder grumbled, but Ethel was too tired to care.

Ethel (center) in high school–shown with two other girls in the mid-1910s.

5

School Marm
1919

After two years of college, Ethel received her diploma in a red satin folder containing a paper with a School Marm gold seal and fancy lettering. Ethel Bruce had become a teacher. Not many girls from Elizabethtown went beyond high school, and only a few became teachers. The date was May 25, 1919. It was a day to be proud indeed!

Mother Lula, wearing a rose colored dress and straw hat, came to the graduation. She stood as straight as a picket fence when her daughter received her diploma.

Ethel's first teaching job was in a one-room schoolhouse, out in the country west of Elizabethtown. In early June, a few weeks after she'd returned home, Ethel announced that she wanted to see where she would teach that fall. Early one morning a buggy pulled by a broad, gray mare, and driven by a Mr. Ames took Ethel out to see the school. It wasn't far from town, but with the rutted road, it took almost an hour before they reached the tiny, white building.

Mr. Ames, a talkative man, whose daughter was in the first grade, told Ethel about everyone that lived along

Ethel's college portrait, probably for the yearbook.

the way. Except for a flick of the reins every now and then across the horse's rump, he let the animal pick where she wanted to pull the buggy.

Ethel clasped her wide-brimmed hat with one hand and the edge of the bouncing seat with the other. She wished Mr. Ames would talk less and direct the horse more.

"The Milton children are all grown but you'll have a boy from the next place." Mr. Ames paused for a moment. "I hope you stay at least one year. Mrs. Mape lasted until the mud got so deep she couldn't get to town as often as she yearned to go," he said. "Then she moved back to

Rosiclare. That's why we asked for an older, man teacher this year."

"Oh, I don't plan on quitting, Mr. Ames," said Ethel. She was bound and determined to last one year. "I don't mind a little mud." She'd show them that she was no Mrs. Mape.

Mr. Ames said, "We'll see," and turned his attention to pointing out another place with school age children. Along the road were small, shabby farms with more hills and rocks than meadows and grass. This part of the county, farther from the river, missed out on the rich soil deposited by the floods. "Mary Hatchet lives there, and she'll be in first grade with my girl," he sighed, "and Nathan Watkins lives down that road."

The buggy lurched across a small creek. On the other side was the school, a simple building with a dilapidated porch in front and three narrow windows along each side. The weathered board siding hadn't been painted in years. A lonesome looking place, thought Ethel. She climbed quickly down from the buggy and hurried up the steps to the porch. She didn't want Mr. Ames to see how disappointed she was.

"Door's not locked," called Mr. Ames, "Go on in."

At the opposite end of the room hung a slate board, a tall stool stood in one comer and the teacher's desk filled the other. Stained and cracked wooden desks faced the teacher's with four in one row for the older students and three smaller desks in the other. Several stacks of books were piled in the comer and yellowed pictures of George Washington and Abraham Lincoln hung side by side on the wall.

Mr. Ames came inside. "You'll have seven students, Miss Bruce."

"Is that all?" asked Ethel.

"That's all, but then Nathan Watkins makes up for three or four." He chuckled.

"Maybe it wasn't the mud but Nathan that sent Mrs. Mape skedaddling back to town."

Ethel eyed the wooden coat pegs by the door, the bench with a water bucket and dipper sitting on it. The school was as poor as the farms. Who would want to teach in this ugly place? It wasn't what she had expected and she struggled not to feel discouraged.

"Please tell me more about Nathan, Mr. Ames."

"Ain't much to tell; he's the oldest one you'll have and a born trouble maker." Mr.Ames changed the subject. "Anything else you want to see before we go? We don't have a teacherage where you can live, so you'll stay with our family September and October, the Hatchets the next two months, and then with some of the others."

Ethel just nodded. What more could she say? They rode back to Elizabethtown in silence.

Summer ended too soon for Ethel. She wondered if she really wanted to be a teacher. She gave up her job helping her grandfather, packed her clothes, and tucked

Harmettio deep in her bag. She hugged Alice and her mother goodbye, and tried to smile when Olive and Daisy dropped by to wish her well. She made sure no one knew how she dreaded leaving Elizabethtown for that dreary country school. Mr. Ames and his mare came once again to take Ethel to her teaching job. There she cleaned the dingy schoolhouse, put alphabet cards above the slate board, hung a map of the State of Illinois behind her desk and placed a vase of wild flowers on a windowsill. Ethel looked around the room with satisfaction. She was ready for school to begin.

The next morning she opened the school house door wide, and even though all seven students were already on the porch, she rang the bell. Ethel immediately liked all the children, but was surprised at how much taller and older Nathan was than the others. She could see that he was their leader, telling them what games to play at recess, what teams to be on, and who was *it* for tag.

Everything went well until the second week of school. That's when it happened!

The porch creaked as the children climbed the steps and scurried into the room.

"Mornin' Miss Bruce," they said in chorus. Some giggled as they took their places. Even Sarah and Mary, the timid first graders, were whispering, as they slid into their desks.

Something's up, thought Ethel. She glanced at Nathan who was leaning back in his seat with his long fingers locked behind his head and a satisfied smile resting on his face.

"Good morning boys and girls." She pulled open her desk drawer to take out the papers she'd graded the day before. As she reached inside there was a loud croak and a large, green frog sprung up before her face and landed on her arm. The children shrieked and squealed with delight. Nathan was the loudest of all. The frog leaped to Ethel's other arm and the students laughed louder, rocking back and forth in their seats. They quickly stopped when Miss Bruce caught the frog in her hands. Turning it side to side she quietly examined it.

"A frog has come to join us," she said in a sweet voice. "How nice! We must learn more about our new friend. Nathan please come forward and please sit on the stool."

Nathan looked confused. He unlaced his fingers, unwound his long legs and shuffled to the front of the room. Everyone was quiet. Miss Bruce didn't scream, or tear out of the door and run down the road. She liked frogs! She really liked frogs!

Nathan stared at his feet as he walked to the corner, swung a leg over the stool, and tried to maintain a cocky air from his perch. He looked at the ceiling, at the floor, and out of the window. He didn't look at Miss Bruce or at the students. The class hero looked plain miserable.

"Croak," he muttered. The boys and girls snickered.

"And what color is our guest?" asked the teacher?

"Green," mumbled Nathan. He stared down at the visitor peeking out between his fingers.

"Is it a big frog or a little frog?"

"A big frog, Miss Bruce."

Over and over, while clutching their guest, Nathan answered the three questions. By noon everyone had grown tired of the frog and the children seemed to know Nathan had met his match.

After school Ethel sent the frog home with Nathan for safekeeping. He never brought it back. From then on Miss Bruce played in the recess games. She ran faster and jumped farther than anyone. She often joined in a game of grabbing a low branch on the oak tree to see how long she could hang there. "Five, ten, fifteen," everyone chanted. This was a different sort of teacher.

Fall faded into winter and soon it was time for Christmas. Ethel couldn't sing very well, but she tried to teach some Christmas songs. Nathan brought in a scraggly tree he'd cut down himself. They made a few decorations, strung some dried berries and hung the paper bells and stars from the few branches. It looked like a poor tree, in a poor school, attended by poor children.

Then Ethel remembered Harmettio. She brought the doll to school and tucked her among the branches. The children were delighted with the blond-haired doll all dressed in blue.

"She's beautiful," said Mary as she gazed up into the tree.

"And she makes our tree a real Christmas tree," added Sarah.

No one mentioned the missing foot and hand and all agreed that Harmettio was just what their tree needed.

In March, when mud season appeared, Miss Bruce didn't quit teaching as Mr. Ames had expected. At recess time all the students, except Nathan, played games on the porch. Nathan tried to run in the sticky, red mud around the trees and buildings. Afterwards he had to scrape his pant legs and shoes with a stick before Ethel let him back inside.

When school let out in May, Miss Bruce moved back to Elizabethtown for the summer. "I'll see all of you in September."

In the fall, she returned to teach a second year at the country school. For her third year of teaching, Ethel and her doll moved to the town of Rosiclare, three miles down the river from Elizabethtown. There Miss Bruce taught twenty fifth graders. She missed her students at the end of the bumpy road and wrote them long letters. A few wrote back.

That winter Ethel met Mike, and a new adventure began.

6

1924

Ethel dusted the window sill and moved Harmettio to dust the top of the dresser. Daisy sat on the bed looking out of the window at the falling leaves. "You just have to go, Ethel. Box Socials are one of my most favorite parties and, besides, the money raised from the sale of the food boxes is going for new library books."

"I'll think about it, but I do have lesson plans to write for next week," said Ethel.

She remembered last year's Box Social when Homer Smith bought her box for fifty cents.

He had complained she hadn't put in dill pickles, and he wanted more sugar cookies. He didn't even like her biscuits. Ethel shuddered.

"Don't you like to decorate a box and see all the different ones others bring?"asked Daisy.

"Last year I made ham sandwiches. I decorated my box with stars and red and white stripes."

Ethel agreed that the flag box was very patriotic. In the end she promised her friend she'd go. On Saturday, she filled a box with fried chicken, potato salad, and apple pie. She wrapped it with white butcher paper from Grandfather's store and tied the box with a royal blue, velvet bow. She tied her hair back with a matching blue bow. It wasn't a fancy box but it would have to do. She was only going to help the library.

When she arrived at the party she hid her box under her arm and, like the other ladies, she secretly placed it on the long table. One box was decorated like a riverboat and another wrapped like a barber pole. Ethel took a seat by Daisy just as the auctioneer held up the first box for all to see. He said, "What am I offered?"

"Two bits," was the reply.

"Thirty cents," called a tall man from the back.

"It smells delicious, like baked ham," the auctioneer announced.

"Forty cents," was the next bid.

And so it went until the bidding stopped. "Sold," said the auctioneer each time a box was claimed. Then he would hold it up and ask, "who's the owner of this fine food basket?"

Daisy stepped forward to claim her box and meet her supper partner. Her box, decorated with fresh flowers and ivy, looked just like a flower garden.

Ethel wondered who would buy her box. Maybe she should have spent more time decorating it. It looked plain and drab. When the bidding on her box began, Ethel's uncle, Dewey, bid twenty-five cents but someone quickly said, "Fifty cents." Ethel turned around to see who the bidder was? She didn't recognize the voice.

"Sixty cents," countered Newton.

"One dollar," was the firm reply. Newton added on a nickel.

"Do I hear a dollar and a dime?"

"Two dollars," was the reply.

Newton looked surprised. The boxes rarely sold for more than two dollars. He didn't bid again.

"Sold," said the auctioneer and he turned to hand the box with the velvet ribbon to the stranger who had come forward. The man with red hair and a ruddy complexion walked straight over to where Ethel was sitting along the wall.

"I know this is your box," he said. "The bow matches the one in your hair."

Ethel blushed as she stood up, "You must be new here," she said. "My name is Ethel and I'm a teacher."

"Yes, I'm new here," he smiled and added, "I'm a mining engineer from Colorado and my name is Mike."

As they shared the box supper, Ethel learned that Mike was building a mill to grind the ore from the fluorspar mines at Rosiclare. While serving the pie, she told him of her life along the river. Before the Box Social ended, they were friends.

When Ethel returned home that evening, she took Harmettio down from the dresser and propped her up with a pillow on her bed. "I met a man from the West," Ethel

Left to right–Ethel's Mom Lula, Mike Cloonan, and Ethel in 1924 about the time of their marriage.

told the doll. "I met a real mountain man, and he was very nice."

It wasn't long before Lula invited Mike for Sunday dinner, and not long after that, Ethel's friends starting calling Mike her beau. As they walked beside the river in the evenings Mike talked about the tall mountains he missed so much. He spoke of the thick forests covering their sides and the icy cold streams that cascaded down from them into the valleys below.

Ethel tried to picture the tunnels and holes the miners dug into the mountains sides. It was hard. She had never been west of her home state and there were no mountains in Illinois. She stopped by the library and checked out books telling of the states beyond the Mississippi River, and of the people who lived there. She read and read but mostly she dreamed of seeing the Rocky Mountains, and Mike's favorite state, Colorado.

The following year when the mining mill was completed, the teacher married the mining engineer. It was a small wedding, Ethel wearing a brown dress with a lace collar and silk slippers. They were moving away to Northern Colorado where Mike had another fluorspar mill to build.

"We'll never see you again," cried Olive.

"I'll come home often, I promise," said Ethel.

Wedding portrait of Ethel and Mike Cloonan.

"No you won't," wailed Daisy. "You're going too far away."

"Of course she'll come to visit," interrupted Alice. Along with Mother Lula, Alice helped Ethel pack the new black steamer trunk with its brass hinges and hasp while her son, Henry, waited to load it on a wagon to take it to the train depot.

Ethel insisted on putting Harmettio in one of the trunk's drawers even though Mike had often reminded her, "We are moving into a two room log cabin. We can't take everything. "

Alice said, "The doll isn't very big and besides, a doll is forever."

Ethel agreed. "Harmettio is going to Colorado."

Amid all the tears, they waved goodbye and Ethel looked back at the Ohio River bathed in a gray morning light. When will I ever see it again?

7

The Journey West

1925

The train sped westward across the bridge, while beneath it the Mississippi River flowed southward. Soon the Mississippi would swallow the Ohio River when they joined some hundred miles away.

Ethel watched from their Pullman car, too enchanted with the new journey to turn away from the window. In the baggage car, to the front of the train, rode the steamer trunk, with Harmettio tucked inside among the clothes.

Before Ethel's eyes a map unfolded, revealing the farms of Missouri, the wheat fields of Kansas, and the prairie of Colorado. What a big country, she thought, and now I get to see it.

On the second day of their trip, as the conductor walked through the car, he announced, "Look out the windows on the left side and you'll see the Rocky Mountains."

There in the distance, below the clouds, tiny snowcapped mountains appeared on the skyline.

A disappointed Ethel said, "I can hardly see them, they're so small."

"They are far away," said Mike. He laughed, "They'll grow, just wait a little while."

And grow they did until they filled the western sky. When Mike and Ethel got off the train in Laramie, Wyoming, Ethel strained to see them through the blowing snow that stung her hands and cheeks. They had no sooner stepped down onto the platform than the conductor signaled to the engineer, and the train roared away. "We can't be too many miles from the mine," said Mike. He looked all around. "We'll take that little train over there." He pointed to a locomotive, two cars and a caboose parked on a siding across a snow blown field.

"That isn't what I'd call a real train," said Ethel "and those don't look like passenger cars."

"This train hauls everything, mail, cattle, timber," said Mike. "The passenger car is the one next to the caboose."

The train that ran from Laramie to North Park.

Ethel shivered, "I wish it would stop snowing."

"It always snows in March," said Mike.

"Back home," Ethel mused, "the trees are budding out." A lonesome feeling swept over her, and she suddenly longed for her family.

"We'd better hike over there and get boarded," said Mike as he picked up their satchels.

Ethel pulled her coat tightly about her. "What about our trunk?"

"The station master will haul it over," said Mike. They crossed the empty tracks and struggled toward the little train. There were no other passengers to be seen. They pressed against the wind and plodded through the snowdrifts. When they reached the passenger car, the steps were down but no conductor appeared to help them aboard or take their tickets.

Inside the car a barrel stove, with a perking coffeepot atop it, stood to one side of the door. It spread welcomed warmth. Mike and Ethel spread their fingers before it and stamped their numb feet.

Several rows of empty seats lined the car and way in the back along with several canvas mailbags stood the trunk. Ethel was comforted to see that Harmettio had joined them. She took a seat near the stove where the car felt the warmest. Then she leaned back, relaxed, and settled down for the last leg of their trip.

Soon three ranchers joined them, and began talking with Mike. Ethel cast about for women passengers to visit

The train in Laramie, Wyoming that Ethel and Mike rode on in 1925.

with, but no one else boarded. Mike asked the men many questions and they readily answered each one. "How far is it to North Park? What did they know about the mine? Had they been there?"

Without warning, the train suddenly lurched forward. Ethel grabbed the back of the seat in front of her to keep from falling onto the floor. They were under way. After an hour, the train began its climb into the mountains. It bucked and jerked as it struggled to go higher and higher. Ethel caught her breath as she looked out over the receding plains. They stretched forever like a wrinkled sheet. She had never been so high. She continued to stare out at the plains until the train entered the forest where the tall trees, laden with snow, blocked her view.

Ethel looked for roads, houses, or barns, but there was nothing outside her window to suggest that people lived in this high world. The hours stretched on. Ethel grew tired of bracing her feet on the seat in front of her to keep from landing on the floor. "Will we ever get there?" she asked her new husband.

"We'll be there in an hour or two," said Mike.

"Where do we get off?" Ethel hoped it was at a town with people and stores. She thought of her Grandfather's general store and, for a moment, wished she were back helping him.

Mike said, "Someone from the mine will meet us. I'm not sure where that will be."

As it turned out the train stopped above a flat area that Ethel guessed was a field.

Willows stuck out of the snow along one edge and meandered up into the canyon. "There must be a creek down there," she said.

Ethel and Mike's cabin at the fluorspar mine at Dean Peak.

Mike agreed.

Beside the train stood a man, hidden in a big coat and wool cap, with the flaps tied under his chin. A sled pulled by a team of workhorses was close by. He shouted greetings over the roar of the locomotive and the wind. He quickly loaded the trunk in the back and helped Ethel into the sled where he tucked blankets around her and topped them with a heavy cowhide. Ethel thought she'd smother under the weight. He didn't waste time visiting but rather tugged on the reins and turned the sled and team around. "I don't want our trail to blow shut," he yelled to them.

Ethel saw a broad valley ahead surrounded by mountains, but soon the sled turned the other way going behind a smaller mountain that Mike called a hill. They entered a narrow valley already darkened by the winter's afternoon shadows. Wedged between the two men and covered with robes, Ethel couldn't see very well. She didn't care. It was such a cold, awful place.

When the team finally stopped, it was before a log cabin, half-buried in the snow.

Mike helped Ethel down and she stumbled toward the door. Inside she looked around the two tiny, mostly-bare rooms. This was her new home. Mike carried in the trunk, shoved it into a corner and went back outside. Ethel opened the trunk, took Harmettio from the top drawer and pressed the doll to her chest. Then she burst into tears.

8

A New Life

1925

Every day, Ethel found more things to cry about. She cried when it snowed and cried when Mike said, "You are the only woman living here at the mine." Forty-nine men lived and worked along the rocky hillside pocked with tunnels and piles of ore. When they saw Ethel, the workers nodded and touched the edge of their hard hats, then hurried on. No one had time to visit with her, no one except the camp cook.

Paul, a small man whose steps faltered and hands shook, was a good cook and a kind person. He urged her to stop by the cookhouse in the afternoon for a cup of coffee. When Paul had the meals ready, he stepped out of the front door of the cookhouse to call the men to come eat. With a long iron rod, he hit the big metal triangle that hung from a chain nearby. A clanging sound rang over the hillside and echoed down the valley. Soon the miners filed into the low wooden building, and sat down at tables covered with oil cloth and topped with platters of steaming food.

Ethel loved hearing the ringing call. It reminded her of ringing the bell at the country schoolhouse not far from Elizabethtown. Each day after lunch Ethel followed the winding path from her cabin down the slope, around some willows sticking out of the snow, to the cookhouse where Paul taught her to play cribbage, a game with a wooden board, pegs, and a deck of cards. As they played, Ethel told him about her family, friends, and the river. Then, after an hour, she wandered back up the hill so Paul could prepare the men's supper.

Ethel looked forward to the cribbage games, but she could hardly wait for the weekly trip to get groceries and the mail at the country store six miles away. To get their supplies, Mike and Ethel rode in a sled pulled by a horse.

Mine campsite looking south at Dean Peak.

A horse drawn sled used for transportation in the winter at the mine.

They frequently got it stuck. Sometimes the sled tipped over on its side. Mike was no horseman and the workhorse seemed to know it. If they were on a hillside, Mike usually turned the horse the wrong way. Over the sled went. Ethel clung to the seat until it came to rest on one long runner that was buried deep in the snow bank while the other runner stuck out above their heads. Then Mike and Ethel rolled out to shovel and push against the sled's wooden side until they heaved it upright. Cold and wet they went on their way.

Ethel liked Ray, the postman and storekeeper. He reminded her of her Grandfather. She became friends with Ray's wife and children, and the ranch folks that lived by the meadows and along the streams. They all talked and laughed as they collected their mail and shopped for everything from work gloves to raisins. When Mike and Ethel got home, she opened the letters from her mother, Alice, and her friends. Then she cried again. Alice always started

Mike and the mine cook Paul in front of the Cookhouse.

her letters, "Dear Ethel, Mike, and Harmettio, We miss you." As she read Ethel sobbed, "I hate this place." But she didn't write about her lonely life or their dark, bare cabin. She wrote about the blinding sun on the new snow and the blue, blue sky.

Mike tried to console her. He simply couldn't understand how anyone could be unhappy living in the mountains.

As the days grew longer, and the spring sun grew warmer, the snow banks began to shrink. One day when Ethel walked down to the cookhouse, she spied tiny yellow flowers blooming along the path. She picked the short-stemmed, waxy blossoms and showed them to the cook. "Look at these beautiful little flowers."

"They're buttercups," Paul said. "They are the first welcome of spring, and soon you'll see bluebells blooming."

Ethel took her flowers back to the cabin. "Where will I put them?" she asked her doll. She smiled as she thought of the perfect vase. She took a thimble from her sewing basket, filled it with a few drops of water and carefully put the buttercups in it. She placed her miniature vase on the trunk before Harmettio.

Ethel said, "I've picked you a bouquet of flowers and it's just your size." The cabin seemed brighter and homier, and she laughed, "I do believe you're smiling today, Harmettio." Then she hurried outside to search for more buttercups.

The following day, Ethel heard a "Yoo-hoo" and opened the door to see a woman, wearing a broad-brimmed hat and riding a tall, white horse rein to a stop before the cabin. Ethel rushed out to greet her. "I'm so happy to see you! Where did you come from?"

The woman said, "I live on a ranch about three miles south of here. My name is Mamie." She dismounted, tied the reins loosely around a nearby bush, and took a brown paper package from a saddlebag. "I brought you a chocolate cake."

"Please come in," said Ethel. "I'll make tea." She didn't know when she'd been so glad to see someone.

They had not one cup of tea but two and a generous slice of cake. Between bites and sips they talked and got acquainted. Mamie had also been a schoolteacher. "I taught all eight grades," she said, "Usually had about a dozen pupils."

"How did you do it?" Ethel asked. She remembered her seven students.

"The young ones learn from the older ones," Mamie replied. Then she noticed Harmettio. "What a pretty doll. Have you had her a long time?"

Ethel took her doll down from the trunk and put her in the center of the table. "I've had her forever. See, she's missing a hand and a foot?" Then she told Mamie all about her life with Harmettio.

Ethel reached for the knife to cut herself another piece of cake. "This is the best cake I've ever eaten." She added, "I can't cook here. Everything is either raw and hard or burned."

"I'll teach you to mountain cook," offered Mamie.

And not only did her new friend teach Ethel how to cook and bake the chocolate cake, but she taught her how to trout fish. They dug worms for bait and cut willow sticks for fishing poles. "The trout are much smaller than the catfish I caught back on the Ohio River, but they're fighters," Ethel whispered to Mamie. Just then a fish struck at her hook, tugged on the line and darted upstream.

At first Mamie brought a horse along for Ethel to ride, but after several months Mike bought her a light-colored mare named Fanny. Ethel fell in love with the gentle horse and Mike was happy to see her smiling again. Waving his arm around at all the mountains, he asked, "Where will you ride today?"

"I'll take Harmettio, and together we'll ride Fanny to the top of the world. It isn't that far away."

During the summer Ethel rode her horse, played cribbage, looked for wildflowers, and made new friends. On the way to the country store, Mike and Ethel waved to their neighbors putting up hay and stopped to watch the youngsters working in the meadows. The children's teams of older horses plodded around and around the familiar fields. They left behind rows of green, timothy hay, waiting to be stacked. Before long, the new haystacks dotted the meadows like green loaves of bread.

"I'm learning the ways of our friends," Ethel wrote to Daisy. "You'd laugh if you could see Harmettio sharing the top of the trunk with my cowboy hat. We've become true western ladies."

Chocolate Fudge Cake
1/4 cube butter
3/4 cup sugar
2 eggs
2 squares Chocolate
1 cup flour
1 tea spoon baking powder
1 tea spoon salt
3/4 cups milk
Cream butter & sugar & eggs one at a time, then melted Chocolate. add sifted flour, baking powder & salt alternately with milk - Vanilla & Fudge frosting

Ice Box Rolls
1 cake Fleishman dissolved in 1 cup warm water.
Cream 1/4 cup sugar 1/2 cup lard & bit mix in yeast
add 1 egg beaten Bake at 375, 20
3 cup flour
mix stiff dough. Place in greased bowl. Set overnight & rise 1 1/2 hours & bake

Recipe given to Ethel by Mamie for high altitude Chocolate Fudge Cake.

9

Hidden Wonders

It wasn't long before Ethel had ridden all the trails around the mine. One day, when she felt brave, Ethel reined Fanny toward the west. Following the ridge, she dropped down behind the hills. A few miles away she saw large rocks stacked on top of each other and strewn over the ground.

Ethel thought, this looks like a child has dumped a huge basket of toy building blocks and never had bothered to pick them up. As she got closer, she realized the giant boulders were like a fortress that stopped intruders from going farther. Within their midst the tops of pine and aspen trees peeked around and above the rocks.

Ethel rode farther, circling the rock pile until she came across a small creek that flowed out from alongside the boulders and into a little meadow. A narrow trail, like a secret path, followed beside the stream. "Oh, Fanny, we have to see where this trail goes," said Ethel. With pounding heart she turned the horse onto the path and disappeared into the granite maze.

Ethel with her horse, Fanny, and dog, Winky.

Hidden inside were grassy open places where cattle grazed, wild flowers bloomed, and birds chirped from the trees. Ethel stopped often enjoying the peaceful scenes. They continue around another rock stack, and to Ethel's amazement, in the middle of the large clearing, stood the ghostly remains of an Indian village. "Oh, my," said Ethel as she reined Fanny to a stop. She stared at the weathered teepee poles still pointing upward. Nearby, a large rock fire ring, blackened by many bonfires, told a story of venison roasting for dinner.

Ethel dismounted and walked around the encampment. A smooth object in the dirt caught her eye. She picked it up, and held a small arrowhead in her hand. One edge was broken off, but the brownish flint was the work of an Indian brave chiseling out an arrowhead. Did it break while being made or was it used to kill a deer? She tucked the arrowhead away in her pocket.

I must ask Mamie about this place. What tribe lived here and when? She mounted Fanny and headed for her friend's ranch.

Mamie knew all about the rock hideout. She called it The Teepees. "Those were the Ute Indians who came here to hunt over fifty years ago." She added, "Let me saddle my horse and I'll show you something else."

They were soon following a road that bordered the meadow. Mamie pointed out a tree in the distance. It grew alone on the top of a hill. "An Indian chief was buried there," she said. "The custom was to bury them among the branches of a tree."

A surprised Ethel asked, "Are the bones still there?"

Mamie laughed, "That was long ago. All that is left are the poles they placed him on. We should find a few beads from his breast plate scattered below."

They tied the horses to the fence posts, crawled under the barb wire, and hiked up to the tree. They could see in all directions, even the rock fortress in the distance.

"It is a pretty place," said Ethel, "but it is forlorn." She stared up into the lone tree.

"They always buried the chiefs facing to the east," said Mamie. "I've never been here when the wind wasn't blowing." She shivered. "Let's look for some beads."

They dropped to their knees to search for the tiny glass beads. They brushed their hands gently back and forth through the sandy soil. Ethel found four pale blue ones while Mamie gave her the two white ones she had found.

When Ethel got back to the cabin, she took the arrowhead from her pocket and placed it on the trunk beside Harmettio. She would give that to Mike. Then she strung the beads on a piece of thread and tied the string behind the doll's head. "What a lovely necklace you have. It is about time I gave you a present from the mountains." She fluffed out the blue skirt, tucked the arm with the missing hand into its folds and pulled the dress down over the leg with the missing foot. Then she carefully sat her doll in the middle of the table.

"Harmettio, I've had such an exciting day."

Ethel with a bobcat at the mine in North Park, Colorado.

10

Ethel's Daughters

1932 - 1940

One fall day when the trees were on fire with colored leaves of red and gold, Mike and Ethel brought home their daughter, a baby girl. They named her Margaret "Lula" after both her grandmothers.

Ethel wrote to Alice, "Harmettio is looking pretty and right at home in the corner of Margaret's crib, but she has to share her place with a teddy bear. It seems like teddy bears are more popular than dolls these days."

Lula made the long trip west to see her first grandchild. Each afternoon she sat on the porch rocking the baby. Soon she said, "I can see why you love the mountains, Ethel.

They take my breath away." Lula stayed until the first snow storm. She promised when she left, "I'll come back when there is a new baby."

Two years later when buttercups and bluebells dotted the ground, red-faced, red- haired, Michala Marie was born. The name Michala was hard to pronounce, and before she was a month old everyone called her Mickie. Once more

Lula came west and once more Harmettio took her place in the comer of the crib. Those who came to welcome the new baby scarcely noticed the old fashioned doll. But she was still an important part of the family as Margaret and Mickie grew up. The girls often fought over whose turn it was to play with Harmettio. One girl pulled on a leg while the other tugged at an arm. Then Ethel stepped in, taking the doll from them and stashing her on the top shelf of the bookcase.

When the girls were six and eight years old, Ethel took them back to Illinois. They met Daisy and Olive and their children and all went on a picnic to a large cave that overlooked the river. As they stood at the mouth of the big cave, Ethel told her daughters, "Many years ago river pirates hid here while they spied on the water travelers. From here

Ethel and Mike in a mountain meadow in the summer around 1932.

they could see far, but those in the boats couldn't see them. The pirates kept their boats hidden along the shore."

The girls looked out over the rocks and bushes at the Ohio River flowing silently by.

They looked up and down the river, and strained to see across it into the state of Kentucky.

Ethel continued, "The pirates waited for boats and barges to rob. The river pilots tried to steer as far as possible away from the bank for they knew all about the cave in the rock." She added, "When I was your age I loved to watch the barges go by and wave to the captains."

"Did you ever swim across the river?" asked Mickie.

"No," said Ethel, "It is a long way and there are dangerous currents."

Margaret and Mickie, Ethel and Mike's children in 1934.

Margaret pointed to the other side, "Then you never knew the people over there?"

Ethel agreed. "It is like living on one side of a mountain and not knowing who lives on the other."

"With a mountain you can climb over it or go around it," Margaret said, "Then you'll meet your neighbors. I think mountains are better to live near than big rivers."

Ethel smiled and added, "You forget that the ferry boat takes people across."

A few days later their grandmother invited friends and family in Elizabethtown to a party to see Ethel and meet her girls. Platters of fried chicken, bowls of potato salad, and baskets of corn bread filled one end of the table while watermelon slices, cake and homemade ice cream in round, wooden freezers lined the other. Alice stood behind the heaping table to help Lula serve.

Ethel hugged Alice. "It's been such a long time. I've missed you every day."

"Every time I help Miss Lula, I think of you," said Alice, "and now I'm so happy you came home and brought your girls." She called to her son, Henry, and his four boys to come meet them.

Henry asked, "Does your mother still have her doll?"

Mickie giggled. "You must mean Harmettio. She's at home. How did you know about her?"

"When I was a little boy I often saw the doll." said Henry. "She was always sitting on your mother's bed."

"Did she still have all her hands and feet?" asked Margaret.

Henry said, "She was brand new then. I didn't pay much attention to dolls, but I remember your mother cried and cried when Harmettio lost her hand."

"She lost one foot too," said Margaret. "It was during a bad flood."

The girls were both pleased and surprised that this tall man remembered the doll, and they all agreed that Ethel should have brought Harmettio back to visit her first home.

Margaret Lou and Mickie almost cried when the party ended, and the girls did cry when they had to tell their grandmother goodbye. "Please come to see us?" they pleaded, and Grandma Lula said she would.

On the trip home, Ethel stared out of the train window. "What do you see?" asked Mickie.

"I'm looking for the mountains," said Ethel. "The first time I saw them they were so far away I thought they were snow- topped ant hills."

The girls laughed at the thought. Ethel said, "Now I know better."

"Let's see who spots the ant hills first," suggested Margaret.

Both girls pressed their faces to the window while the train clattered and swayed back and forth. They didn't notice the plains that rushed by as the three of them watched the far western horizon.

"There they are! I can barely see them," Margaret exclaimed.

Mickie added, "I see them, too."

"They've been waiting for us to come home," announced Ethel.

The second fluorspar mill built by Mike in the 1940s.

11

Poor Harmettio
1940

They hadn't been home long from their journey east when Mike bought a tall, upright piano. He wanted his daughters to take music lessons. Years before, the trunk was shoved out of sight and Harmettio was moved to the bookcase. Now she had a new home on top of the polished, brown piano. Before long a new doll, about the same size, joined her.

Margaret was given a Storybook Doll for her birthday. Dressed in pink satin and trimmed with lace, the doll, called Sunday's child, made Harmettio look plain and dowdy.

Staring at the two dolls, Margaret said, "Harmettio needs a new dress. We should make one for her."

"A good idea," said Mickie, "but we don't sew very well. I don't even know how to sew a button on a blouse."

Margaret said, "How hard can it be? A doll's clothes are so small they must be easy to make."

The girls gathered scissors, thread, and needles. They cut away Harmettio's faded blue dress and laid her on the

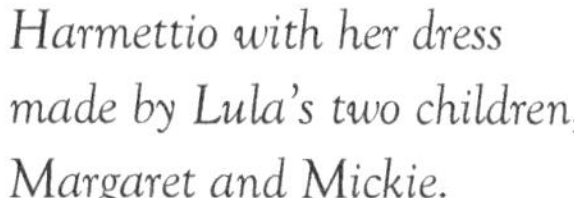

Harmettio with her dress made by Lula's two children, Margaret and Mickie.

table. From their mother's scrap bag they found a piece of mustard-yellow material with tiny purple dots on it. Margaret spread out the square of cloth, folded it in half and Mickie placed the doll on top of it. Harmettio's body, made of rough burlap cloth, looked very old and out of place against the bright print.

"She's kind of funny looking," observed Mickie, "Let's hurry and cover her up."

They traced around the doll with a black crayon to make a pattern. They left lots of material for the skirt and then cut through the two pieces to make them exactly alike. One piece was for the front of the dress and the other piece for the back. Next they sewed the two pieces together. "I can hardly wait to see how Harmettio looks," said Margaret, "Let's put it on her before we hem the skirt."

She tried to pull the dress over the doll but her head was too big to go through the hole they'd left for the neck. Margaret tugged and pulled on the material until Mickie came up with an idea "Why don't we sew the seams up with Harmettio inside?"

Margaret agreed and got to work cutting out the stitches so they could start over.

They struggled to hold the doll, the material, the thread and the needle. Their stitches grew bigger, looser, and in many places the brown body showed through. At last the front and back were sewn together and Margaret held up Harmettio for inspection in her new yellow dress.

"She doesn't look very good. The sleeves are too short, and there is something wrong with the front of her skirt," said Margaret.

At the mine in North Park in 1943.

"Let's add an apron to cover up the pucker in the front," said Mickie as she searched through the scraps until she found a small square of dark purple fabric. "This is perfect," she said and handed it to Margaret Lu who tacked it on. But even the apron didn't help Harmettio's new outfit. Margaret was tired of sewing. "We should have left her alone. She looks terrible."

They decided to put the doll aside and do something else. Sewing wasn't much fun, and besides, it was obvious they needed their Mother's help. "We'll make her another dress soon," said Mickie, and she climbed onto the bench to put Harmettio as far back on the top of the piano as she could reach. No one could see her there. Then they forgot about her.

Several days later when Ethel was dusting, she lifted the Storybook Doll with her one hand while she swished the thick, wool dust cloth across the wood.

Crash!

Ethel peered behind the piano and there lay Harmettio. Scattered around her were the tiny glass slivers of what had once been the doll's only hand. Ethel pulled Harmettio up from the floor, examined her dress and dangling arm. "Now you have no hands, and where did you get that awful dress?" she asked. She sighed as she gazed at her doll and ran her hand over Harmettio's yellow glass curls. "I shouldn't have let the girls play with you." Ethel held the doll out before her. "You are still a pretty lady to me. You're still my doll."

Ethel carried her doll into the bedroom, sewed together the empty stump, and wrapped her in tissue paper. "Poor Harmettio, I don't want to hide you but who knows what will happen next" She gently put her doll in the bottom drawer of the old dresser. "Poor Harmettio," Ethel repeated, as she turned away.

Ranch house near the mine.

12

Forgotten Doll
1974

"Where have the years gone?" said Ethel as she pulled open a bottom dresser drawer and began going through it. "I can't believe I've had seventy-five birthdays." Her daughters were grown up and had moved to Denver, one to become a teacher and the other an accountant. After thirty-five years of marriage Mike died. Ethel continued to live among their friends and her mountains.

In time she became a grandmother; but no one thought to prop Harmettio in the comer of her granddaughter's crib. Instead a mobile of wooden clowns, elephants, and monkeys swung and whirled above the bed. Ethel rocked the baby in a brand new rocking chair and hummed her favorite old-fashioned songs, sometimes singing, "She'll be Coming Round the Mountain." And when her grandsons were born she sang to them, "I Ride an Old Paint."

After a while Ethel grew lonely and decided to move into an apartment closer to her daughters. Margaret and Mickie came home to help her pack.

Ethel lifted a brown and green shawl from the dresser drawer and spread it out on the bed. She examined the simple pattern of the crocheted shawl that her mother had made for her. The yarn was a little faded but it looked quite new since Ethel hadn't worn it very often. It was difficult to hold onto a shawl in the windy mountains. Why that was over fifty years ago, she thought as she reached for a pair of long underwear, yellowed with age. Ethel chuckled, "Mother Lula sent the shawl and underwear when I moved to Colorado. She thought it was always winter here."

Ethel put the shawl back in the open drawer and tossed the woolen underwear into a cardboard box placed on the floor to hold the items to be thrown away.

"You won't need all these linens, Mother," said Margaret as she came into the room with an armful of blankets and sheets. "I'm putting them in the giveaway box."

Ethel nodded, "I'm so glad you and Mickie came to help me. I hardly know where to begin." She reached to the back of the dresser, felt something stiff, and pulled out her doll.

Ethel feeding Chee-Chee, the family's pet deer in 1943.

"Would you look at this? Look, Margaret, here's Harmettio! I can't believe my eyes!" Ethel held her doll tightly for a moment then handed her to Margaret saying, "It has been a long time, too long."

"I see she's still wearing the dress Mickie and I made." Margaret laughed, "The dress was supposed to be beautiful but we didn't know how to sew. Did you ever see anything so ugly?" She called down the hallway, "Mickie, come look! Mother still has her doll."

The three of them examined the old doll and Mickie said, "No hands, only one foot and wearing that horrible dress. You'd better put Harmettio in the throwaway box."

"She doesn't look that bad," protested Ethel.

"The only good part of her is her head," said Margaret. "Remember you aren't going to have a lot of room in an apartment."

"Why don't you keep something that isn't broken?" suggested Mickie, "Take more old photographs or books."

Ethel looked down at her doll. "She isn't very big."

"She is worthless," Mickie said, "I'll bet you couldn't even find hands or a foot to repair her."

Ethel reluctantly put Harmettio in the throwaway box and they all went back to sorting and packing. Ethel opened the closet door and pushed back the hangers to see her clothes. Now why did I save that gray blouse? I never did like it. She dropped it into the box, covering her doll. She held up each skirt, blouse, slacks and dress, selecting about half of them for her suitcases. The rest were tossed into the giveaway or throwing away boxes until they both overflowed.

About then Margaret called, "Are you ready for me to haul out the boxes?"

"In a few minutes," Ethel replied. She sat down on the bed feeling old and tired. She thought of the many adventures she had with Harmettio. Ethel bent over to rummage in the box until she found her doll. She spoke softly, "Alice always said a doll was forever and, besides, you are still a Pretty Lady to me." She held her doll until she heard Margaret coming. "I can't give you up," Ethel whispered. She quickly took out the shawl, wrapped it around Harmettio, and shoved her back into the dresser.

"Are you getting tired Mother?" asked her daughter.

"I was," said Ethel "but I'm feeling much better now." She didn't mention that Harmettio was moving with her. That was their secret.

12

A Playmate
1983

Della arrived at Ethel's apartment one snowy winter day. "I'm here to clean for you," Della announced, "And this is my daughter, Carrie. You did say it was all right if I brought her?"

Ethel had called for a cleaning woman to help her out. "Of course," said Ethel, "I'm glad both of you have come. I even have some toys that belong to my grandsons. You can play with them, Carrie."

Della went to work dusting and vacuuming while Ethel pulled from the closet a basket filled with wooden blocks, a metal toy dump truck, and a small bulldozer.

"How old are you, Carrie?" asked Ethel.

Too busy to talk, Carrie held up three fingers. She tipped the basket to spill blocks all over the kitchen floor. Then she lifted out the bright yellow bulldozer and with both hands lowered its blade to push the blocks into piles.

"I hope you like my toys," said Ethel as she folded and carried some towels to the hall closet.

"Rum, rum, rum," hummed Carrie as she drove the bulldozer, shoving a pile of blocks alongside the table leg and another pile in front of the stove. Next she filled the dump truck with blocks and hauled them to a corner of the room.

But it wasn't long before Carrie grew tired of pushing blocks. She stacked them up into two tall towers and went to find her mother. "I wan'na help," she told Della who was dusting the bedroom, "I wan'na clean! I wan'na jump on the bed!" Ethel heard the questions and called, "Do you want to see my doll?"

Carrie thought that was a fine idea and came running. "You're old," she said, "Why you got a doll?"

"Oh, I don't play with dolls anymore but this is the doll my mother gave me when I was a little girl." Ethel took Harmettio from the drawer and held her out for the child to inspect.

Carrie studied the doll. "Her head's hard. She's got no hands. Where's her foot? She doesn't look like a doll."

Ethel showed Carrie how to hold the doll. She began to tell her all about Harmettio.

"My doll was like other dolls with hands and feet until one night when I was chasing fireflies. "

"What are fireflies?"

"They are flying bugs with little lamps in their tails that go off and on." Just then the phone rang and Ethel hurried off to answer it.

"Be gentle with the doll," called Della.

Carrie held the doll as she was shown. She squeezed one arm and a leg and turned Harmettio upside-down. Holding the doll that way she went into the kitchen, sat down on the floor, and began to play.

After a few minutes Della heard a terrible commotion and ran to the kitchen. She got there just in time to see Carrie swinging the doll around by her skirt. Carrie aimed the whirling Harmettio at the blocks. As the doll's head slammed into the tower, blocks shot out across the room. Bang! Boom!

"Carrie," shrieked Della. She grabbed the doll from the child's fists.

"I made a crane," said a proud Carrie, "See it hit?"

Della carefully inspected Harmettio while she sternly told her daughter, "This is a doll and you don't treat a doll that way." Then she sighed, "You've been playing with your brothers too long." Della sat the doll on top of the refrigerator, told Carrie to put the blocks in the basket, and went back to work.

When the apartment was spanking clean and it was time to leave, Della told Ethel, "Carrie knows about trucks, bulldozers, and cranes but she doesn't know about dolls, especially those with china heads. You had better keep your doll out of sight."

Harmettio went back into the drawer never to be a crane again.

13

Harmettio Anew
1994

DENVER

Ethel died when she was ninety-five years old. Once more, her daughters sorted, packed or threw away Ethel's belongings. They knew they wanted to save her favorite cookbook and a cracked leather photo album filled with loose pictures, and tattered pages.

"Here's Mother's baby picture," said Margaret, "and one of Grandmother Lula on a picnic. See the thick braid wrapped around her hair. "

"How about this one of you and me on our stick horses?" said Mickie, "Look at the baggy long stockings we wore."

It took them over an hour to study all the photographs in the old album. "If we take this much time on every item we'll never get finished," said Margaret as she jerked open a dresser drawer. Glancing inside she announced, "There isn't anything worth saving in here."

Mickie helped her pull out and turn the drawer over the throwaway box. Out fell an old shawl that landed with a soft thud in the box. Mickie said, "There's something wrapped up in there." She grasped a corner of the shawl and gave it a shake. Harmettio tumbled onto the carpet!

They stared at the doll in disbelief. Margaret picked her up studying the long forgotten Harmettio. "I thought Mother threw her out."

"I was sure she had," said Mickie. They were silent for a few minutes. "She kept her doll all these years. Mother must have loved Harmettio more than we ever imagined."

Margaret nodded, "We can't throw her away." Then she laughed, "If she just didn't have that awful dress."

Mickie added, "And we know who made it. Imagine spending nearly fifty years in a dress like that. She's a very old doll and deserves something nice to wear."

Margaret had an idea, "Let's get someone to make a pretty dress for Harmettio?"

Mickie agreed, "And if we could find hands and a matching foot and..."

Margaret, who was always the practical one, interrupted, "The doll is almost a hundred years old. I doubt if we can find a foot to match and who knows what the hands looked like."

"It's not like she is some kind of rare and expensive doll," said Mickie. "I imagine Great-grandfather Birch sold all kinds of them in his general store."

Margaret said, "We won't know without some research."

"I'll go to the library when I get home," Mickie said. She hurried from the room to find a shoebox for Harmettio's trip back to the mountains.

While Mickie searched for clues, the doll stayed in the box on the top shelf of a closet. What had her hands looked like? Who made the doll? And more important, who could repair Harmettio? Mickie found the answer when she saw an advertisement in a doll lover's magazine. On the top of a page was an advertisement that read, "We never saw a doll we couldn't make like new. Bring your broken dolls to THE DOLL HOSPITAL."

Mickie and Harmettio entered the door of a shop along a shady Denver street. Inside were shelves and glass cases filled with broken dolls with cracked heads, scratched faces, missing eyes and who knows what else was wrong with them. Mickie whispered to Harmettio. "You'll fit right in."

A woman in a white, cotton coat, just like the doctors sometime wear, stood behind the counter gluing a yarn wig with long pigtails on a tall doll. "Hello," she said. "Do we have a new patient?"

Mickie opened the shoebox. "This was my mother's doll, Harmettio."

Taking Harmettio from the box, the doll doctor inspected her. She held one arm, carefully turning it in her hand.

"My mother said she stepped on Harmettio's hand when she was catching fireflies."

"Hmmm," said the woman, "and where was that?"

"It was along the Ohio River in Illinois." Mickie asked, "Is she fixable?"

The doll doctor didn't answer. She looked at the remaining foot, felt the stuffed cloth body, and asked, "May I cut her dress off?"

Mickie nodded, "Although it was my mother's doll, my sister and I played with her.

We made the dress," She hurried to add, "when we were very young."

The woman smiled. Snip, snip, and the dress lay on the counter. "May I cut here?"

She pointed to a place on the doll's cloth body, right below the breastplate.

Mickie agreed, and after two or three tiny cuts, sawdust began falling into the shoe box. "We'll put the sawdust back in when we sew her up," the woman said as she felt in the hole. "Hmmm," she murmured, "Just as I suspected, the breast plate has a small piece broken off. This doll must have fallen off of something."

"The piano," filled in Mickie. "She lost the other hand when she fell."

There was a long pause while the doll doctor studied Harmettio. Then she announced, "We can make her like new." She turned to take a big book from the shelf behind her. After flipping through the pages she found what she was looking for. "Isn't this your doll?"

Mickie held her breath as she looked down the page filled with pictures of china headed dolls. "This one, this is the one!" Mickie shouted. She pointed at a doll with tiny, cupped hands and feet with painted brown shoes and blue garters. "Except for black hair she is exactly like Harmettio."

"These dolls were made in the late eighteen hundreds and early nineteen hundreds," said the woman. "The heads, hands, and feet came by boat from Germany. When they got to America the bodies were made and stuffed. The head, hands, and feet were attached, and they were dressed. They weren't expensive dolls."

"She means a lot to my sister and me," interrupted Mickie.

"Of course," said the woman, "A doll is forever."

Mickie could hardly wait to call Margaret. She asked the doll doctor, "How long until she is fixed–I mean until she's well?"

"This will take a while." The doll doctor began measuring Harmettio, "We'll send off to have the hands and foot molded, and we'll make the dress." She wrote down the measurements. "It will take at least six months."

Mickie left Harmetio in the shop, drove home and waited, and waited. After seven months she could wait no longer and called The Doll Hospital. "Is my doll ready?"

"Her hands haven't been sent as yet." she was told. "They must be specially made, you know," the voice said.

Mickie tried to be patient. "No news about Harmettio," she wrote to Margaret. "It has been ten months."

After nearly a year Mickie received a postcard. It read, "Your beautiful doll is well and ready to go home."

No more dresser drawer for Harmettio. She stands tall and regal in a glass case on the piano. The tall windows across the room frame the mountains that rise higher and higher. In her long light blue dress with wee, white dots, long sleeves, and a full, lace- trimmed skirt that hides two matching glass shoes, she looks like a brand new doll. Beneath the dress, lace-edged pantaloons meet the two blue garters. Harmettio is once more a Pretty Lady.

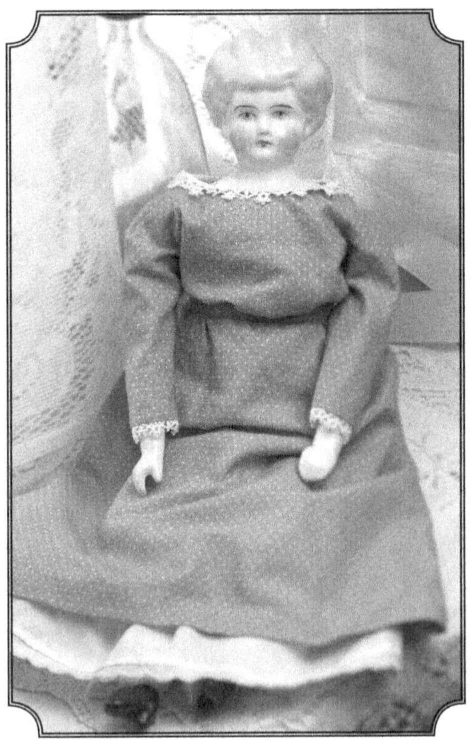

Harmettio after being restored and with a new dress.

Epilogue

Mickie died on August 6, 2012. Harmettio is now a treasured family heirloom belonging to Paige Miller, Mickie's only granddaughter.